handwritten: x/v 264

handwritten: 99p

WALKS

IN

EAST HAMPS

G000126298

By

Brenda M. Parker

Photographs by Dick Amey

New edition with updated routes and maps
Published June 1990

Cover: The Church at Buriton

Opposite: The Church at East Meon

SBN 0-86146-027-8

PAUL CAVE PUBLICATIONS
LTD

in conjunction with the Hampshire Area, Ramblers' Association.

Printed by Brown and Son (Ringwood) Ltd.

FOREWORD

The foreword to the first edition of this book told of the difficulties of following many of the paths in the English Countryside. I am pleased to report that there have been many improvements since then in East Hampshire, particularly in the provision of stiles and signposts, for which we have to thank our District and County Councils. You may still encounter problems with ploughing and crops, and I am sure Brenda's carefully written descriptions will give you confidence in choosing the correct route. I hope you will not find any of them illegally blocked by long lengths of ploughed surface, oil-seed rape or waist high corn sodden by recent rains, to name some of the horrors that can be encountered.

Brenda's selection of routes in East Hampshire will take you through some of the best scenery in this outstandingly beautiful part of the County, and walking them should encourage you to explore the area still further on foot.

Michael Clark

Vice-Chairman, Hampshire Area, Ramblers' Association

Opposite: The Church at Hambledon

3

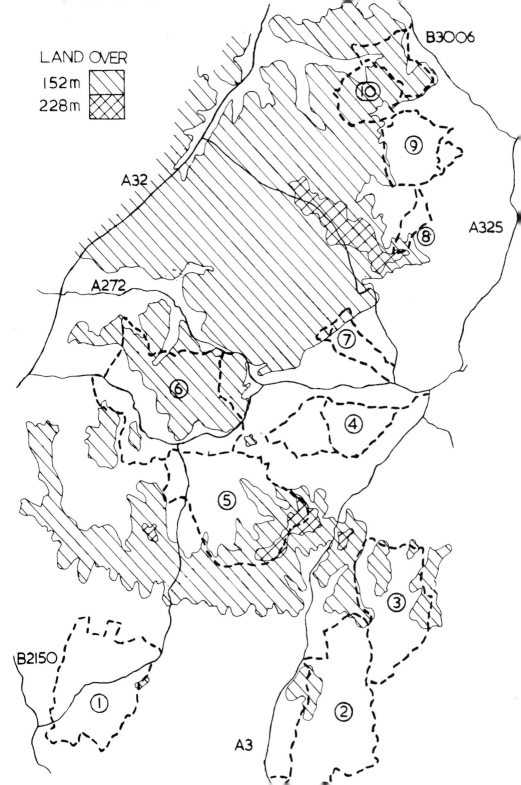

INTRODUCTION

All the walks described here are circular, and were written with cars in mind, not because I wish to encourage even more cars to use our overcrowded roads and those few lanes where it is still possible to go safely on foot, but because there are so many beautiful, and peaceful, places which cannot be conveniently reached by public transport, especially on a Sunday. In two of the villages, East Meon and Hawkley, space is limited and the parking recommended is a few minutes walk from the start of the walk.

Although each walk is complete in itself, as can be seen from the map opposite, many of the walks interlink or can be made to do so quite easily. For anyone who might wish to turn several into a larger circular walk — or even walk the full 'outer' route of 47km (30 miles) from Horndean to Selborne via East Meon — there are connecting maps at the end.

The maps and text between them are enough to guide you round the walks but they are necessarily rather limited and much more information on the surrounding countryside can be gleaned from a 'proper' map such as the Ordnance Survey 1:50000 (Landranger), or better, the 1:25000 (Pathfinder). All these walks are on sheets SU61/71 (1285), SU62/72 (1256) or SU63/73 (1244).

When I wrote this book in 1976, many of the paths used were not visible on the ground. Whether their subsequent appearance was my doing, I do not know, but appear they have. However, there still may be difficulties — stiles wear out with use, hedges grow sideways — so please report any that you find to East Hampshire District Council or to the Ramblers.

The Ramblers' Association is concerned not only with walking and protecting rights of way, but also with all aspects of access to the countryside. Further information may be obtained from: The Ramblers' Association, 1/5 Wandsworth Road, London, SW8 2XX.

Brenda M. Parker

KEY TO MAPS

═══	Surfaced Road
⋯⋯	Unsurfaced road, track or path between boundaries
⋯⋯	Fence, hedge or other boundary
🌲	Woods, of any sort
∿∿	River or stream
⟩⟨	Bridge
✚	Church
PH	Public house or inn
P	Parking place
■	Building, occupied
□	Building, unoccupied or barn
△ •	O.S. trig. point, spot height. All heights in metres.

All distances are in metres or kilometres (miles). A typical walking speed is 4 kilometres per hour (2½ m.p.h.).

All compass directions on maps show magnetic north.

PLEASE KEEP THE COUNTRY CODE

Enjoy the countryside and respect its life and work.
Guard against all risk of fire.
Fasten all gates.
Keep your dogs under close control.
Keep to public paths across farmland.
Use gates and stiles to cross fences, hedges and walls.
Leave livestock, crops and machinery alone.
Take your litter home.
Help to keep all water clean.
Protect wildlife, plants and trees.
Take special care on country roads.
Make no unnecessary noise.

WALK 1

HAMBLEDON

Northwards past the Vineyard, over Windmill Down to Chidden, the cricket field and Broadhalfpenny Down — 13km (8 miles).

Start: Hambledon village, grid reference SU 647151. Cars can be parked in the main street or in the lane by the George Inn. No official car park.

From the main village street, go up the rise to the church and through the gate into the churchyard. At the back of the church turn right along the tarred path to the road. Cross almost straight over and take the lane by the school.

To visit the Vineyard, go straight along the track which soon becomes a grassy path between fields above the hidden village, and turn left at the drive.

For this walk, which passes above the vineyard, go through, over or round, the field gate on the left just past the allotments. From here the path rises diagonally to the trees on the skyline. If the path should not be visible on the ground, aim not for the stile you can see in the right hand fence, but for the left-most tree. This line should bring you to a fence corner from which the stile at the gateway in the skyline hedge is visible. Go over this and follow the hedge on your right over the crest of Windmill Down. The several stiles may or may not have fences attached. At the road cross over on to the tarred drive signed 'Bridleway'. Just at the end of the hedge on the right there is a stile. From this cross the field to the corner of the wood. Now follow the wood edge along the ridge and over a stile, a fence and rails into a grassy track between hedges, gaps in which give occasional glimpses over Chidden Holt on your right. At the road turn downhill to the hamlet of Chidden, turning right at the road junction. The road is at first unfenced. At the first hedge on the left, go through the gate and up the field edge with the hedge on your left. This field, over 1km (¾ mile) long by ½km wide, is Chidden Holt. Shortly after two rusty water tanks, there is a metal footpath sign and a gate with a stile. Climb over this into a grassy lane which becomes a tarred road at the farm. At the junction turn right to the foot of the hill (Beware — this road is rather narrow). Opposite a track on the left, go over a stile into the field and turn south along the headland with the fence on your left over a stile back into Chidden Holt.

(The roundabout nature of this last kilometre is due to the way the rights of way network developed, with paths radiating out from the village rather than running east-west. There is no official right of way connecting the track end and your present point.)

Turn left along the headland and shortly left over the stile into the copse. The path winds and eventually emerges on the north side into the field. Turn right along the headland to a gate and stile at the road. Cross leftwards to a field entrance and then bear right over the stile. The cricket ground is at the top of the down in front of you. To reach it, turn left along the headland and over the stile, turn right and keep with the fence over three stiles on to the road. You have now crossed to the opposite side of the valley which contains Hambledon village. Turn right to the memorial to early cricket and 'The Bat and Ball'.

At the cross roads on the far side of the inn, turn right (busy road) and keep on the left hand verge to a stile opposite the side road. Climb up the field to the corner of the wood on the skyline to a good track rising gently up the edge of Broadhalfpenny Down with extensive views to the west and north. Once round the corner, the track becomes a shady lane between hedges passing a survey column on your right. This must date the hedges since the view from it is now nil! The occasional views through gaps include Windmill Hill two ridges away to the east (Walk 2).

Past the Watertrough

At Scotland, the tar starts. Immediately after the cottage turn left on to a path between hedges. This eventually emerges on to a cart track. Here turn right and then left at the clearing. Although all these tracks are shown as roads on the maps, only those from the west to Glidden are actually tarred, those to the east all being cart tracks. At the next junction turn left again. Just past the barn, keep right on the track open on its east side to the field falling into the valley. The view ahead ends with the ridge of Portsdown 8km away. Just past the small copse on the left turn right down the field edge and the south edge of Greatsteds Copse. After the dip, head straight across the field past the watertrough. A gap in the hedge leads to a track through the wood and out over a stile into a field on the edge of a dip. Keep left round the edge of the wood and up the slope to a track. Follow this left to a minor road which leads right to Rushmere. At the junction follow the road left and right.

Opposite a wood on the left climb the stile and follow the field edge to the tree belt. Once over the stile into the trees, turn right over another stile onto a path enclosed between the wood and a fence. Here, at last, you begin to get a glimpse of the village in the valley bottom. Over the stile turn downhill and then bear right along the pasture to a beech tree and so through an iron kissing-gate on to the road. Turn left downhill to the village.

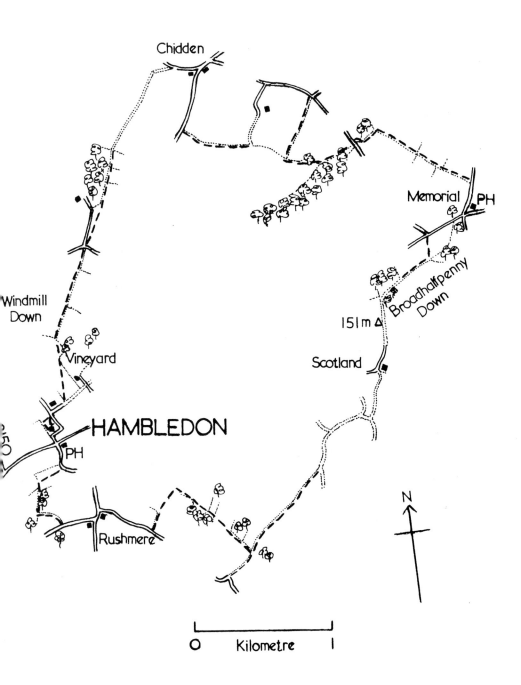

Chidden

Memorial   PH

Broadhalfpenny
Down

Windmill
Down

151m △

Vineyard

Scotland

HAMBLEDON

PH

Rushmere

N

0   Kilometre   1

WALK 2

HORNDEAN

East and north to Chalton, Queen Elizabeth Forest and Windmill Hill — 14km (9 miles).

Start: Horndean car park, grid reference SU 708132. The car park is signed from the Rowlands Castle road, just beyond the A3 junction.

On leaving the car park, turn right up a shady road and follow it to Blendworth where a footpath sign points to the right down a track between the houses. Go through the gate at the end and keep along the fence through the field to a stile on to the road. A few yards to the left go over another stile by the cottage and again follow the fence over three fields to a stile on to another road. Again turn left and at the corner climb a stile and follow the field edge. At this next road, do not cross straight over but turn left and then right following the road round the outside of the woods of Idsworth House. When the road begins to go down the hill and bends left, take the bridletrack on the right which gently descends the face of Wick Hanger. At the bottom, past a notice warning against damaging trees and shrubs, the path becomes a lane emerging on to the road opposite Wick House. Cross straight over and start the long climb up the cart track on to the summit ridge of the down. Gaps in the hedges give occasional glimpses of the valleys and surrounding downs. At the top of the hill, by a narrow wood on the right, turn left over the stile in the barbed wire fence and along the track on the field edge by the wood. In the valley to the east lie the railway and the site of the original Idsworth, of which virtually all that remains is a chapel in the middle of a field and part of the manor house. As you round the corner of the wood, the summit of Chalton Down comes into sight on the left. Before reaching the gateway in the next fence, go over the stile on the left. This path is very well used and will probably be trodden out. If it is not, head past the pylon to the right hand side of a grassy mound (tumulus, or barrow) on the skyline. Here you should pick up the direction down the other side from the waymark post. If further guidance is needed, set off in the direction of the gate straight ahead right down the hill until you get to the flat. When you can see a stile by a gate in the left hand hedge head across to it and cross the pasture to a stile into the churchyard extension, and a gate ('Sheep working. Shut gate please.') into the churchyard proper. The 'Red Lion' faces the church across the village green.

For the next 1½km (1 mile) the route is common with Walk 3. Leave the village past the telephone box and along a track between buildings. Past the farmyard go over or through the gate on the left (not up the track to the right) and follow the hedge steadily uphill towards the forest. Level with the pylon, climb the stile on to the right hand side of

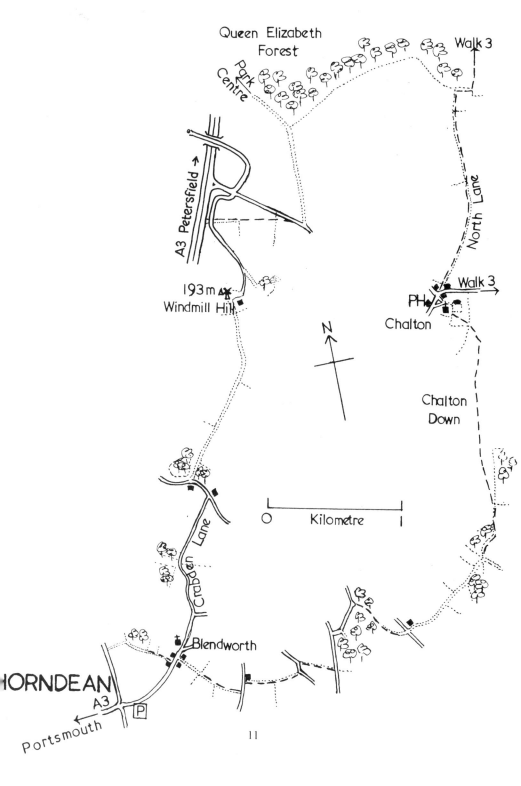

Queen Elizabeth
Forest

Park
Centre

Walk 3

North Lane

A3 Petersfield →

193 m ▲
Windmill Hill

N

Walk 3

PH
Chalton

Chalton
Down

Kilometre

Crabden Lane

Blendworth

THORNDEAN

A3

P

Portsmouth ←

"Sheep Working" sign on the churchyard gate at Chalton

the fence and continue upwards to the forest edge. Here turn right down the field edge to the stile, a narrow path bringing you on to the forest ride. Turn left and keep by the forest edge over the hill, joining the horse trail, and down the valley bottom to the corner of the wood above a wide valley. To visit the Park Centre or link with Walk 5 on Butser, turn right. (Supplementary Map A.)

To continue this walk, go through the gap and turn left along a track between fences to the road. Here turn right and very soon climb the stile on the left. The path crosses the field corner diagonally to a fingerpost in the cross fence. From this, bear slightly left and uphill aiming for the corner of the hedge. Once safely up the rise keep by the hedge to the stile on to the new access road to Windmill Hill Farm. This is not a public right of way. Cross it to a second stile, turn left along the verge of the A3 for about 20 metres to another stile which takes you back on to the access road. This will take you up the hill to the restored windmill (not to working order, though). On the way up, turn round for the view back to the forest and the downs. At the top, turn away from Chalton and the windmill and go south past the house, through a gate and down the grassy track that drops gradually between fences or hedges back towards Horndean. At the road turn left to New Barn. (The verges on this road are wide enough to allow parking and offer an alternative starting point.) Opposite New Barn take the lane on the right (Crabden Lane) back to Blendworth. Here you can either retrace your steps down the road that you started out on or, as an initially more pleasant alternative, take the path opposite that you took originally. Through the yard, go over the stile into the field and straight ahead to a track through the wood, turning into a narrow path between fences and descending to the A3.

12

WALK 3

CHALTON

Ditcham Woods, Chalton and Queen Elizabeth Forest — 11km (6¾ miles).

Start: Forestry Commission car park above Buriton, grid reference SU 733198.

Leave the car park eastwards, away from the Forest, following the South Downs Way, which here is a deep-cut lane between coppiced hazels. Almost at the top of the rise, a gap on the left gives an extensive view north-west over Petersfield to the hangers. Keep on the road, past Dean Barn, and on to a rutted chalk track with occasional views southwards. At the point where the track first bends left you are directly over the main Portsmouth railway line, buried in its tunnel some 100m below.

After winding over two hills, the track drops down to become a road at Coulters Dean Farm. At the corner where the road turns left, take the bridleway on the right, along the lower edge of a nature reserve. Please heed the notices. Through the bridle gate out of the reserve, the path is unfenced in a wood of young beech and climbs steadily bearing to the left. At the cross-track go straight over, turning right at the ride on the edge of the wood. Where the ride bends right downhill, go left through the bridle gate and over the brow to a road and a good view of the ridge of the downs. Turn right and follow the road to a junction of tracks where you take the gravel track straight ahead which leads downhill past Ditcham House. At the deserted cottages, the track becomes grassed over past the neglected wood but improves again on emerging into the open between fields, and descends to the road at Woodcroft Farm. Cross straight over the road following the footpath signpost, through the farmyard to a gate in the railway fence, and over the footbridge. Turn left at the road and very soon right up the path by the fence of Woodcroft House. Once over the stile into the field climb the steep rise by the wood until the stile in the centre of the fence becomes visible. From the stile, you should aim across the field for the telegraph pole. When a second pole appears on the right, head for this instead to the stile, which lies just to its right. (If walking in the opposite direction, the fingerpost gives the correct line.) Turn right down the road into Chalton.

Here the route joins that for Walk 2. At the first road junction, turn right between the cottages, past the farm buildings and over or through the gate into the left hand field. The path, the now-invisible North Lane, keeps on the left of the hedge uphill towards the forest. After the gap near the pylon, cross by the stile into the right hand field and continue up to the edge of the wood. Here you have to turn right down the field

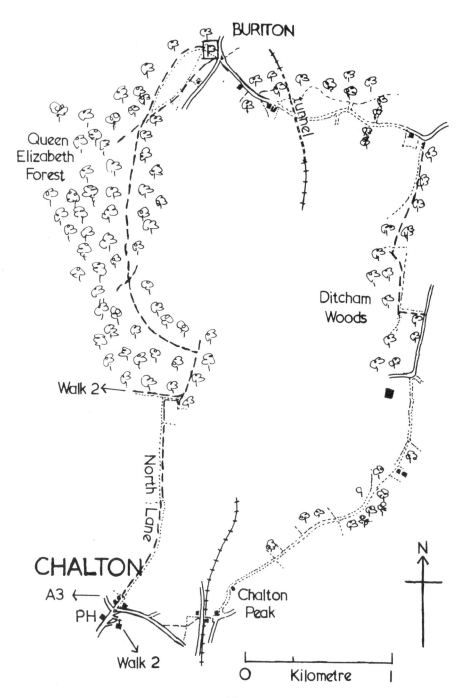

BURITON

Queen
Elizabeth
Forest

Tunnel

Ditcham
Woods

Walk 2 ←

North Lane

CHALTON

A3 ←

PH

Walk 2

Chalton
Peak

N

0   Kilometre   1

14

Buriton Church

edge to find the stile giving access to the Forest. A short, narrow path leads on to a broad ride. Follow this northwards. At the first junction bear left. Ignoring all side tracks and horse trails, keep onwards more or less on the level. At the 'major' junction cross over on to the track climbing ahead. On the left you soon pass some former experimental tree plots. (There are more on War Down.)

Eventually the ride descends to a junction with a horse trail at a point where the track is on the top of a very narrow ridge. About 50m further on, just before your track joins another, wider one, turn right down a path through the trees to a bridle gate and a stile. At the field keep by the left hand bank through the gap into the field behind the cottage. Diagonally across this to the right is the stile back into the car park.

(The path in Ditcham Woods was diverted early in 1977.)

15

WALK 4
PETERSFIELD

South west to Stroud and Ramsdean — 7 or 10km (4½ or 6 miles).

Start: Petersfield market square. No parking on Saturday, market day. Large car park off A272 and A3. Grid reference SU 747233.

Leave the market square by the south west corner, by the church. At the other end of The Spain, keep to the left of the hospital along a path which used to be a road. Cross the railway and turn left and then right through the industrial estate. At the end of the road turn left along an enclosed path to a stile and bridge over the stream. The path through the newly extended industrial estate is signposted — keep by the stream and round the corner, then turn left between buildings, across the access road and over a stile. Bear right across the field to a stile in the far corner. (The Petersfield bypass is to be constructed across here in the near future.) Over the stile, follow the farm track until you come into a large field with the farm at the far end. From the gateway bear left across the field to the hedge corner, then turn right to a stile. Over it, turn right, past the farm. Keep the same line across pastures and several stiles until the last one brings you into the end of a lane. At the western end of this, the long and short routes divide.

For the longer route via Ramsdean, cross the road and climb a stile into the pasture. Bear slightly to the left to a gateway on the left of a clump of trees. Turn left down the lane which becomes a grass track once past the cottages and brings you out eventually into Ramsdean. Turn left, and left again at the road junction. In about 400m (¼ mile), turn right down a track which becomes deep cut and drops steeply round a corner to cross a stream and then climbs again to meet a concrete farm road. Turn left up this and follow the waymarks. Just before the farm, bear right and go through the left-hand of a pair of gates. Following the hedge first on the right and then the left, you come out on to a farm track. When this bends left keep straight on across rough ground, over a stile and so into the road, at Weston. At this point you join the shorter route.

For the shorter route to Weston, turn left down the road from the school. At Stroudbridge take the track on the left past the house leading to a field gate. Head towards the farthest left corner of the field (on right of wood). Through the gate into the wood, the track leads uphill to the road at Weston.

Follow the road past Weston Farm and take the track on the left by the cottages. After the last cottage, the path turns left out of the sunken track over a stile into the field. Turn right, downhill and over a stile into the 'cattle track'. From this, turn right through a gateway into the large field on the right which stretches down to the railway. The stile out is in the far right corner. At present the path follows the edge of a triangular field to an underpass leading to an enclosed path and the road. In future, you

16

will have to cross the Petersfield bypass again before the underpass. Keep straight on up the road and back to the square.

This walk links with Walk 5 at Ramsdean.

The view towards Queen I

Forest from Windmill Hill

WALK 5

EAST MEON

Small Down, Hyden Hill, Butser, Ramsden — 11½km (7 miles).

Start: East Meon village, grid reference SU 681221. Parking in the village is limited, especially during church services. There is good parking on the road south, about 5 minutes walk from the village.

From the village centre take the road west, parallel to the main road. At the crossroads turn left. Just after the road bends right and past the last house on the left, cross the rough car park to a stile. The path rises up the field to a stile at the hedge corner then follows the hedge to its next corner before taking off downhill across the open field to the corner of the tall hedge in the bottom. Follow the hedge. At the end of the next field a stile leads on to a track. Follow this sharply uphill and once through the gate turn left along the hedge, along the flank of Small Down. At the end of the field a track drops eastwards through a gate. Turn left down this into the lower field and keep by the left hand hedge to the road.

Cross the road and bear right to a drive entrance. Immediately at the corner climb the stile and take your direction from the fingerpost across the pasture to the corner by South Farm farmhouse. Go through the farm yard and down the track which leads past the source of the Meon towards the down. After passing a barn and going through two gates, climb up, initially on a good track, to join the ridge on Hyden Hill

This track (part of the proposed South Downs Way extension to Winchester) runs right along the summit ridge eventually becoming a road at the house. At the crossroads turn left. This road leads to Butser hill and can be busy at weekends. However, its verges are of reasonable width.

Butser is now part of the Queen Elizabeth Forest Country Park and parking is *not* free (toilet facilities near the relay station).

At the entrance to the Park a track branches left and is the slightly shorter way of leaving Butser. For Butser summit carry on through the cars to the relay station. From the Ordnance Survey column on the summit aim north west over the down and go through a gate in the fence corner. Descend the ridge of Ramsdean Down with splendid views to the north. At the wood go through a gate into the lane and so to the road. The road straight ahead leads to Ramsdean and connects with Walk 4.

But for this walk turn left, first right and left on to a gravelled track

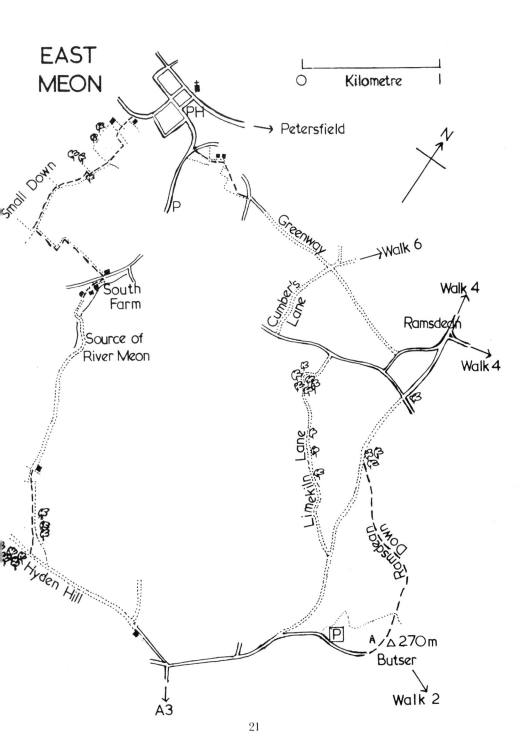

EAST MEON

○ Kilometre |

→ Petersfield

PH

P

Greenway

Walk 6

Small Down

South Farm

Source of River Meon

Cumber's Lane

Walk 4

Ramsdean

Walk 4

Limekiln Lane

Ramsdean Down

Hyden Hill

P

A △270m

Butser

Walk 2

A3

The little street known as the Cross in East Meon

(Greenway). At the 'roundabout' take the second exit and continue on. (This part is now the reverse of the start of Walk 6, which turns north at the junction.)

At the road go almost straight over, up a grassy rise and over an awkward bar stile. Cross the pasture heading for the left-most house to a bridge over the stream (River Meon!) with stiles at each end. The path leads in front of two houses to a stile, across a field and over another stile into the recreation ground and hence back into the village.

Back at Butser, Limekiln Lane forms a very pleasant alternative to Ramsdean Down. Turn left at the start of the Park and keep left on the ridge. (The extremely steep path into the coombe is not recommended.) At the road turn left for about 400m (¼ mile) and then take the track on the right to the 'roundabout'.

WALK 6

EAST MEON

Pidham, Lower Bordean, Old Down and Westbury 14½km (9 miles).

Start: East Meon village, grid reference SU 681221. Parking in the village is limited but there is a good space 5 mins walk to the south on the Clanfield road.

The first mile of this route reverses the end of Walk 5, starting off across the recreation ground to the east of the village. At the far side go over the stile, across a field and over a second stile. Past the houses a concrete bridge with two stiles gives on to pasture. Bear right across this to a bar stile in the furthest corner and down the bank to the road. Take the lane almost opposite (Greenway). This soon becomes a grassy track. At the open space where several tracks meet, keep left into Pidham Lane, ignoring Woodbridge Lane which branches off very soon on the left. At the road, turn right. At the road junction follow the bridleway sign past the cottage, through the gate and into a sunken lane along the field edge. This rises gently to a bridle gate at the foot of the wood. Now take the gravel track which rises steeply up a small valley cutting back into the down. At the top turn for a view of Butser and then right under the pylon line down a good track between fields to the main road at Lower Bordean.

Turn right here if you wish to link with Ridge Top Lane (Walk 7) — Supplementary map B.

Turn left along the road (good verge) and left again at the side road. At the first field gate on the right, a bridleway sign points across the dip. The path follows the hedge up on to the down. At the trees, cross into the left hand field and on to a track between the buildings and Mere Pond. This descends between fields to the drive of Tigwell Farm. Turn right to the road, cross straight over it and take the lane opposite. At the crossroad turn right to Old Down Farm. Keep below the buildings on to a gravel track (signed) which descends between first fields and then parkland and a wood, leading at the bottom through a gate into a field. Keep by the hedge to a gate on to the road.

Turn left past Peak Farm to a gate on the left with a footpath signpost. The path drops to the corner of the wood and then rises to the right along the wood edge to a gate. At the top of the hill at the wood end, go through the bridle gate on the left. Descend the hill by the fence then hedge on the right with a view over to Westbury and Hen Wood. At the old field boundary the path goes through the gap by the wood. Further down you pass through the end of a wood and along another field edge to the stile on to the road. Turn right along the road for ¼km

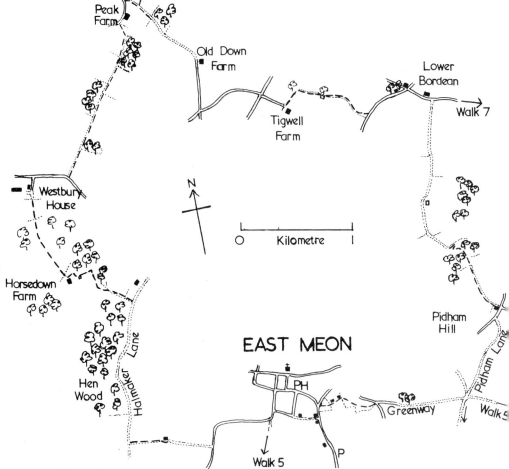

(300 yards). This road is inclined to be busy and does not have good verges, so take care.

At the white-gated drive to Westbury House, go up the drive keeping left past the high wall to an iron gate giving on to scrubby pasture. A track rises into the woodland and through two gaps in cross fences. After the second it becomes grassy and leads up the dip towards a wood on the left. At the corner there is a stile and a jump. The path goes below the garden of Horsedown Farm to the field edge at the shed, and thence down the field edge by the fence. At the bottom drop down the bank on to the forest ride and follow it to the right. When it bends right at the brow of the hill, keep straight on for a little and then climb the stile on the left into the field. From here drop steeply down over two stiles into Halnaker Lane which winds to the right past the edge of Han wood.

When a farm comes into view on the left, go over the stile towards it, through the gate and down the concrete track to the road (stile at the house). Turn left for East Meon.

WALK 7

PETERSFIELD

North west to Lythe Hanger and Stoner Hill — 8½km (5¼ miles).

Start: Petersfield Station, grid reference 743236. Parking see Walk 4.

Leave Petersfield by the A272 (Winchester) road, going west. By the last house on the right follow the footpath sign pointing to Lythe Hanger. After about 200m (216 yards) on the gravel track a second sign-post points over a stile and across the fields. The next three stiles are visible from each other.* Once over these, keep in the dip in the centre of the field to a footbridge with stiles at each end. Over the stile at the other side of the next field, aim just to the right of the house on the hill until you can see the field gate. Turn left down the lane.

Cross straight over the road and over the stile. At the corner of the right hand fence, you will see the next stile in the gap in the left-hand hedge. Continue over the iron footbridge and stile. The next two stiles are slightly to the left in the field corners. At last, Lythe Farm comes into view on the rise in front of you. Aim across the next field for the left side of the house (the track on the right of the field is not a right of way). Once over a brow you can see the next stile in the bar fence by the gate. Leave the last field by the gate in the far left corner. (This makes a total of 12 stiles and two gates in under 2km (1 mile)! The rest isn't so bad.)

Go straight along the track by the barn. Where the track emerges from between hedges, turn left between the fences (do not go into the field in front of you). At the foot of the hanger there is a choice of ways. To the left a deeply-cut track leads steeply up the hill. This is much used by horses and is very unpleasant when the ground is wet. Alternatively, scramble up the bank on your right and over a low stile. From here a narrow path slants up through the plantation. Whichever path you choose, turn right at Ridge Top Lane at the top of the hill. When the lane joins the road, bear right.

At the end of the hedge on your right, go through the field gate and descend the hill keeping by the hedge on the left. At the foot a stile leads into the old beech wood and the path drops to the right to a forestry road. Follow this to the right for a few yards until you can see the stile in the corner of the field at the foot of the hanger. Your way now lies across the middle of the field to the jutting corner of the hedge, over a stile and into a shrub-dotted pasture. Cross this diagonally and follow the left hand hedge to the road. Beware of the soft ground round the hidden spring in the centre of the field.

On reaching the road, you will see a footpath signpost to your left. Follow its direction over two stiles and cross the drive of Colyers. Go

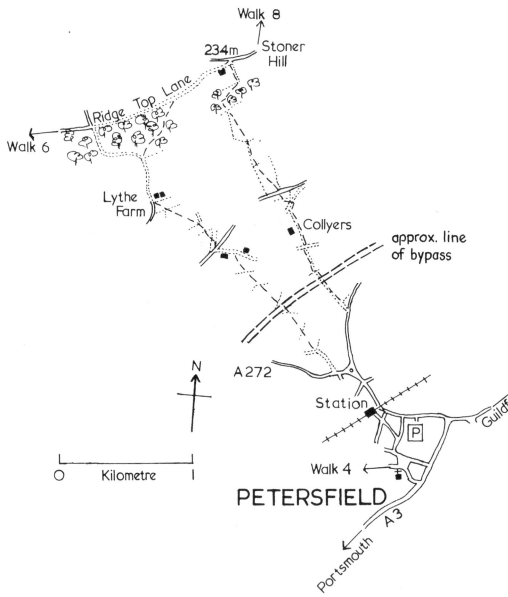

Walk 8

234m   Stoner Hill

Ridge Top Lane

Walk 6

Lythe Farm

Collyers

approx. line of bypass

N

A272

Station

Guildf

O   Kilometre   1

P

Walk 4

PETERSFIELD

Portsmouth   A3

through the gate on the other side and turn right along the field edge. Keeping the same direction on alternate sides of the hedge, a line of * five stiles bring you out into the road which leads to the right back to Petersfield station. This last path ends with a footpath signpost indicating Stoner Hill.

Ridge Top Lane provides the connecting link between this walk and numbers 6 and 8. (Supplementary maps B and C.)

Opposite: The view back towards Lythe Farm

* Petersfield bypass will cross about here.

WALK 8

HAWKLEY

Southwards to Wheatham Hill — 5km (3 miles).

Start: Hawkley Church, grid reference SU 746291. Parking in the village is limited, but the Liss road to the east has wide verges.

From Hawkley Church take the 'No Through Road' going south. Past the large house this becomes a track, inclined towards mud, leading over the Oakshott stream and then bending uphill towards the hangers. From the top of the hill there are fine views to the south.

At the road, turn right and almost immediately left up a gravel track. This soon bends to the left and climbs the flank of Wheatham Hill. The clay here can be very greasy after rain. On the ridge, it is joined by another track which has climbed the shoulder of the hill. Turn right and shortly climb a stile by a gate on the right. Cross the pasture, keeping to the left of a small wood, to the lower edge where the ground drops steeply into the hanger. Turn right, and keep by the fence, over a stile by a gate of poles and over a second stile by a hunt jump into a rough pasture. Turn half-right and descend to a stile at the top of a pasture. From here there is a superb view northwards to Hawkley Hanger and Noar Hill.

Descend the pasture to a stile. Over this the path is confined to the edge of the field by a fence which guides you round to a gravelled parking area. Turn right down a lane between the houses. At the road at Middle Oakshott Farm go slightly right over the road and climb the stile into a long, narrow, wet pasture. When the grass track bends right and uphill, keep left near the stream. In the far left corner of the field, cross to a stile and a plank bridge. From this cross the pasture to a pipe bridge, a stile and a plank bridge in quick succession, and enter an area of scrub. Go uphill to the bottom of a wooded hanger, and turn right along this. Cross a stile into scrubby pasture. Continue along the valley side, crossing a stile, passing above a fenced dell at a dip and over another stile to a footpath junction beside the garden of the house ahead (3-way signpost). Turn left, uphill, cross a stile and continue up a fenced path at the edge of a field. Cross the stile at the top and turn left along the concrete track leading down to the road on which you set off.

This walk is superb in the spring.

From the track on top of Wheatham Hill it is possible to continue southwards to connect with Walk 7. (Supplementary map C.)

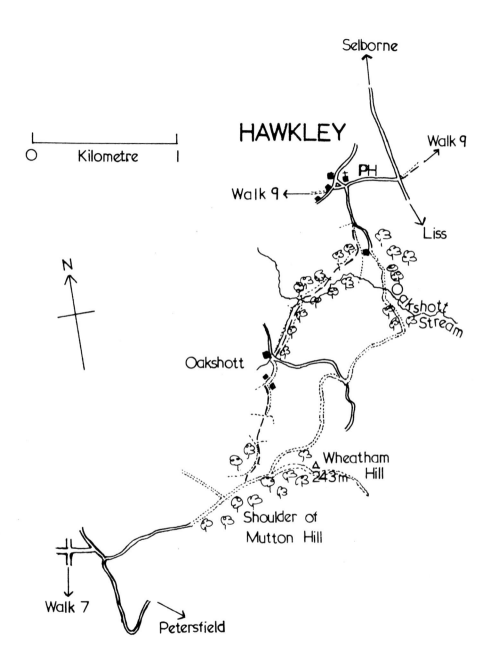

HAWKLEY

Selborne

Walk 9

PH

Walk 9 ←

Liss

Oakshott
Stream

N

Oakshott

Wheatham
Hill
△ 243m

Shoulder of
Mutton Hill

Walk 7

Petersfield

O　Kilometre　1

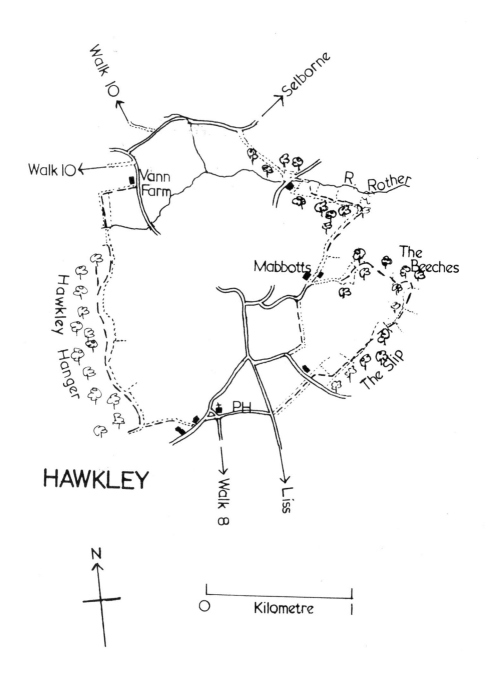

Walk 10

Selborne

Walk 10

Vann Farm

R. Rother

Hawkley Hanger

Mabbotts

The Beeches

The Slip

PH

HAWKLEY

Walk 8

Liss

N

0   Kilometre   1

WALK 9

HAWKLEY

Hawkley Parish Church

The Slip, The Beeches, The Rother and Hawkley Hanger — 4 or 8km (2½ or 5 miles).

Start: Hawkley, grid reference SU 746292. Parking in the village is limited. Some of the roads round the villages have wide verges.

From Hawkley Church take the road past the Hawkley Inn. At the road junction cross straight over, over the stile and along an enclosed path ending in some rails. Turn right at the road and almost immediately left to a gate and stile by a fingerpost in the hedge. Cross the field to a stile in the corner, then follow the top of the hanger through two field gates. Shortly after the second, cross a stile on the right into the wood. A good path descends through the hanger (The Slip) with a gate followed by a double stile at the bottom. The path now follows the bottom edge of the hanger fenced off from the pasture on the right. At the end of this, the path goes back into the wood and bends left round the hanger's foot through The Beeches. There are yellow waymarks at intervals on posts or trees. After a stile skirt the top edge of a small bracken-grown clearing, cross a stile, descend a short way through woods and cross another stile into the top corner of a pasture. Here leave the hanger at last and drop down to a gateway and stile where a track is joined which crosses a stream and then climb the hill to Mabbotts.

For the shorter walk, turn left here on to the road. At the corner climb the bank to a bridlegate and sign-post. Follow the left hand field edge to a gate on to the road. Turn left past Uplands to retrace your route along the enclosed field path and hence back to Hawkley.

For the longer walk turn right and pass between sheds (not up drive) into a lane which at first contours then drops between high banks to a gate and into a pasture. Follow the now grassy track as far as a slight rise and a group of pines. Here go left over a stile and follow the lower, sign-posted, path through a strip of wood and over a stile into a series of three rough pastures (ancient meadows). Keep on the left as near the wood as you can, crossing stiles at the intervening fences. At the end of the last field go through the gate and over the stile which you can see on the right. This leads to a path between fences in a wood and over a footbridge crossing the young River Rother. At the road, turn right as far as a track on the left which climbs a steep bank. This leads between fields to another road. Here turn left and keep on the road, over a ford (another branch of the Rother) where the specially waymarked 'Hangers Way' is joined. Leave the road by a stile on the left, cross the field, over a stile, and continue along a field edge (Battery hens to right), then over the stile on to the road, where Walk 10 is briefly joined. Turn left, past Vann Farm and enter the first field on the right at a stile and two fingerposts. Go along the field edge away from the road, cross a stile and continue round two sides of the next field, turning left in the corner at a two-fingered post. Before reaching the next corner pass through a gap on the right and immediately over a stile into a short length of fenced path. This soon descends a steep bank to the nascent River Rother (on a day in the autumn in 1976, the spring was right under the bridge). At the top of the other bank the path joins a well-used bridleway and is inclined to be muddy. Stay on the bridleway round the hanger foot past the back of Hawkley village. Pass through a gateway on the left and along the field edge with the hedge at first on the right and then, after going through a gateway, on your left. The track finally leads out into the service road behind the houses and back to the village green.

A walk for the autumn when the trees are bare and the views through them less restricted.

Opposite: The village of Selborne from the famous Hanger

WALK 10
SELBORNE

Noar Hill, Buttons Lane, Holtham Lane and Selborne Common —
7km or 10½km (4½ or 6½ miles) with variations.

Start: Public car park behind Selborne Arms, grid reference SU 744332.

Leave the car park by the path to the Zig Zags. At the foot of the
hanger don't go through the gate but turn left along a path which
emerges between gardens on to a road. Turn right and immediately take
the left fork. Before the last house turn left down the gravel path between
gardens to the main road. Turn right along the footway on the other side
of the road and walk out of the village. Just past the road junction is a
well in the right hand bank erected in 1879 and dedicated to Gilbert
White. Just to the left of it, there is a field gate by a metal footpath sign.
Keep on the right hand edge of the field heading south. When the field
edge bends sharply to the right, turn half-right and cross the field to a
gap in the hedge. Turn left along the field edge, over the stile in the
corner. This is waymarked. Ascend over the field to a stile in the next
hedge then up the edge of the field by the hedge to a stile into the beech
woods of High Wood Hanger.

Turn left along the bridle path following the foot of the hanger,
passing a sunken lane on the left, resisting the temptation of any tracks
going uphill until you have reached the south side of the hill and a track
joins from the left. The wood here becomes more mixed with yews
among the beeches, and the path rises through them round the face of
the hanger. On the top the Hangers Way joins from the right carry on on
the level to just past a gate into a field on the right and a multiple path
junction.

For the shorter walk turn right here on to a bridle path which becomes
narrow between hedges, drops and then rises into the open scrubland
pitted with chalk diggings. At the bridleway T junction, turn left and
drop down a good track passing through a gate (Nature Reserve notice)
and continuing between hedges to the road. Turn left and almost
immediately right to the Selborne-Newton Valence road. About 300m
(300 yards) to the left a track on the right marks the join with the longer
alternative.

For the longer walk, from the path junction on Noar Hill ignore the
first left (Hangers Way) and take instead the second bridleway, initially
level along the top of the hanger. At a second junction, after a glimpse of
a field on the right, take the track which drops steeply down to the
hanger foot and leads out between hedges on to a narrow road. (At this
point, you join the route of Walk 9.) Turn right along the road and then
left at the junction. Past the broiler (?) houses turn right up the very
steep and stony track. This is Button's Lane, now worn in parts into a
narrow groove by the combined efforts of motor cycles and water. Where

it levels out on the brow of the hill, the walking becomes easier (I once found a Mini jammed in the track hereabouts!) and soon the track becomes a tarred road. Stop at the road junction and look back over Noar Hill and Selborne.

Cross over on to the gravelled Holtham Lane which winds between hedges. Ignore turnings first on the right and then almost straight ahead instead bearing right downhill through the wood to the road. At the road junction ahead, walk towards Selborne for about 300m (300 yards) to join the shorter walk at the track which climbs northwards on to Selborne Common.

At the top of the hill several tracks meet. If you wish to descend the Zig Zag path take the one on the right on the hill top. For better views turn right downhill to the edge of the wood. At the wood corner a stile leads into a field on the right. Follow the headland to the left to a gate and then across the top of the pasture to a stile on to a concrete drive. Turn downhill. The drive becomes a tarred road which will soon brings you back to the car park.

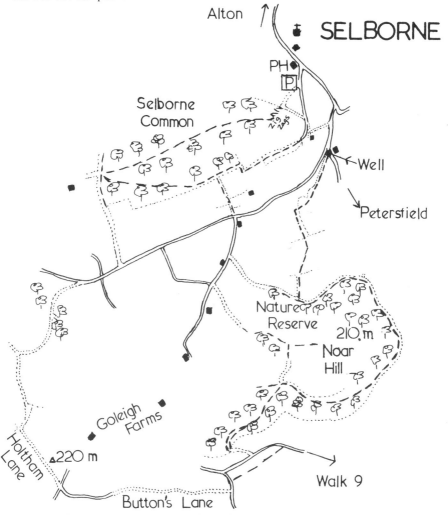

Alton

SELBORNE

PH

Selborne
Common

Well

Petersfield

Nature
Reserve   210 m

Noar
Hill

Goleigh
Farms

Holtham
Lane

220 m

Walk 9

Button's Lane

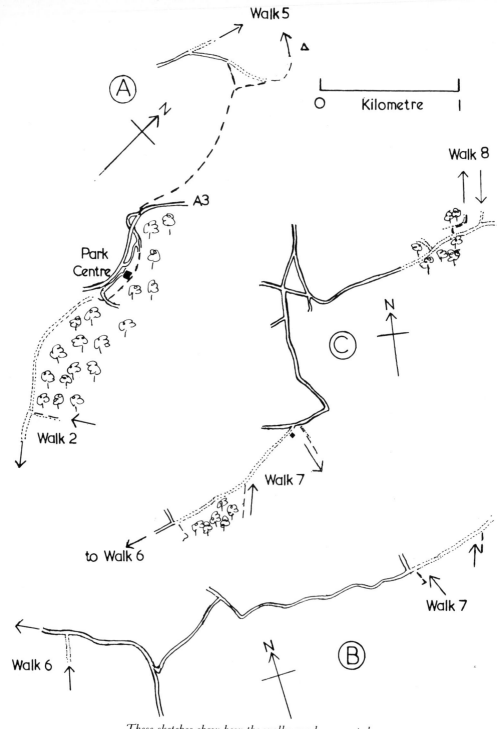

These sketches show how the walks can be connected